ABOUT TIME!

Reflections From the Heart And Mind Of a Prize-winning Poet, Author and Christian Minister

By

Harry J. Fielding

Go with God!

Harry

I YF 2005

© 2003 by Harry J. Fielding.
All rights reserved.

No part of this book may be reproduced, stored in a retrieval system, or transmitted by any means, electronic, mechanical, photocopying, recording, or otherwise, without written permission from the author.

ISBN: 1-4107-2705-X (e-book)
ISBN: 1-4107-2706-8 (Paperback)

This book is printed on acid free paper.

1stBooks - rev. 02/27/03

INTRODUCTION

The title of this collection is intended as a double (or perhaps more accurately, triple) entendre. In its simplest sense, the title refers to the passage of time in which the author has lived. In this sense the issues and events are "about" this passage of time. The poems range from simple verse, to humor and philosophical reflection. Several poems have been published previously in different anthologies, but this is the first time the poems have been gathered together in this way and this is the first collection of poems which are entirely my own to be published. A draft collection of these poems was previously circulated under the title **Perspectives**, but the present collection has been revised and some new poems and two essays added.

A second "meaning" of the title is found in the nature of some of the poems contained. Poems such as **Genesis, Meditations On A Sleepless Night, Bygone Days, After Hiroshima, Death Of My Father,** and **Child Of The Future,** to name just a few, contain philosophical reflections regarding the impact of time upon individuals and events.

The third and possibly most important nuance is intended to sound a wake up call. This is reflected in one of my latest poems, which bears the same title as the book. That poem was written in response to my participation on Saturday January 18, 2003 in a "Peace March" in Washington DC. Millions of people in the United States and around the world also marched on that day, to send a message to politicians around the world that it is "about time" that they began to consider and implement alternatives other than war and violence to solve the major problems that the world faces. As well-intentioned as President Bush might be, clearly the majority of the world's people do not agree with his intended directions. A recent major poll in Europe found that 85% of Europeans saw the United States as the greatest threat to world peace. We stand on the brink of warfare, and by the time that this book is published we may already be at war. I can only hope and pray that common sense and reason will prevail. And if we are at war by the time you read these words, I urge you to join with me in ensuring that in future we will only resort to warfare as an absolutely last resort.

We live in a relational age. If the major economic superpowers would spend even one tenth of the money that they squander annually on producing defense systems and "weapons of mass destruction" (which are okay for THEM to produce, apparently, but not okay for those with whom they have disagreements) and would instead seriously address the social and economic problems which beset the majority of the world's population, then perhaps the time would come sooner than we might expect or might dare to hope for, that the world might live in peace.

It's About Time to try some new directions!

CONTENTS

                                        Page:

INTRODUCTION iii

BEGINNINGS: 1
  *   Genesis 3
  *   Meditations On A Sleepless Night 5

WAR and PEACE 7
  *   Negotiation 9
  *   Settlement 12
  *   Bygone Days 14
  *   After Hiroshima 15
  *   About Time 17

REFLECTIONS on DEATH 19
  *   James K. Baxter 21
  *   Swan Song 23
  *   Obituary for HJF 26
  *   Death of My Father 28
  *   The Garden 30
  *   Tribute to Columbia 32

NEW LIFE 35
  *   Incarnation 37
  *   Daybreak 39
  *   Regeneration 40

IN LIGHTER VEIN 41
* Sunset on Lake Wanaka 43
* Haiku 44
* No Convenient Country Churchyard ... 45
* The Journey 47

JUSTICE or JUST US? 49
* Perspectives 51
* A Search for Meaning 52
* Child of the Future 53
* The Proposal 55

TWO ESSAYS 57
* I Believe 58
* Just Jesus 90

ABOUT THE AUTHOR 113

ABOUT TIME!

BEGINNINGS

The opening poem was written during my student days at Auckland University in New Zealand. I was converted to Christianity in my mid-teens and grew up happily on a diet of fairly orthodox Christian beliefs. I left school at 15 years of age, partly as a result of the trauma in our family at the death by accident of my sister Shirley who was 3 years older than me, but largely because the expectations of my working class parents were that I would earn some money to contribute to the family coffers. At 19 years of age I went on a working holiday to Australia and lived with the Burdekin family. Brian, the eldest son, was then attending university in Melbourne and went on to become the president of the Student Association and in later life was a Human Rights Commissioner with the United Nations.

The Burdekins challenged me to develop my mind, and upon returning to New Zealand I attended night classes and gained my university entrance qualifications. I enrolled at university and like many a young person before and since, found my traditional

Harry J. Fielding

Christian beliefs sorely challenged. **Genesis** is as much a symbolic statement about my own awakening as it is an attempt to deal with metaphysical beliefs.

The second poem in this section is a simple piece of nostalgia. It was written after I had graduated and was entering the teaching profession as a primary (elementary) schoolteacher. I had also accepted the responsibility of serving as a lay pastor of my congregation.

ABOUT TIME!

GENESIS

That was a dawning!
I stood there on that first, eventful morning
And watched the gradual fading of the night.
I gazed, and saw the sun's first rays appear:
They came in answer to the summons clear:
"Let there be light!"

The light was good!
Spirit spoke to Spirit as I stood
Enraptured—joy was manifest!
For in this light all lives are edified:
When fervent, groping souls are unified,
Then, Spirit ends its quest.

The day was born;
Rejoicing in the knowledge of that glorious morn,
Yet still I wonder—was it quite
Like that, or was it all a dream?
For time has passed, and it would seem
We now love darkness more than light.

Now the day is dead.
The brave, yet transient light has fled
And darkness reigns once more—

Harry J. Fielding

The arctic night
Has come, and in perpetual dark
We hide; our world is stained with stark
and loveless blight.

The sky grows pale.
Eternal morning, waiting to assail
The reigning darkness, taps impatient feet.
Truth grows ever restless in the womb:
Gives rise to pains—when light disperses gloom,
Then, birth will be complete!

ABOUT TIME!

MEDITATIONS ON A SLEEPLESS NIGHT

Yesterday,
The smell of cows' dung
And the warm milk
Spurting from pliable tits.
Yesterday,
The warm wind
Tangling my hair
As I raced astride Pinto,
My Pinto,
Across the simple world,
The understandable world
Of yesterday.

Today,
The sober reality
Of responsibilities
Understood and accepted.
Today,
The decisions
That will create
The yesterdays of tomorrow.

Harry J. Fielding

    And tomorrow?
    And tomorrow?
    "The moving finger writes
    And, having writ
    Moves on…"

    And tomorrow?

WAR AND PEACE

Vietnam. The war that no one won. The war that should never have been. The war that divided households and communities. The war that spawned unprecedented protests and demonstrations around the world. I marched in many a "demo" while at university, including protests about Vietnam and protests at the perpetuation of the apartheid segregation system in South Africa.

The first three poems in this section deal with Vietnam. Younger readers will perhaps not know the significance of the "round table" reference in ***Negotiation,*** a solution arrived at after months of bitter haggling as to which country should be represented at the "head" of the table. The ancient symbolism of the legendary King Arthur's table is picked up again in the third poem, ***Bygone Days,*** although it is an implied rather than an overt reference.

The fourth poem in this section is timely, although it was written not too long after the other three. But as I write these notes, the

Harry J. Fielding

United States and her allies stand on the brink of war with Iraq, and civil wars and terrorism are rife. It is not just Iraq that threatens the long-term existence of the world, but all countries (including those of the western bloc) that continue to manufacture and proliferate weapons of mass destruction. This theme is picked up in the last poem of this section, **About Time** from which the title of this book arises. It was written in response to my participation and that of my teenage son, James to a Peace March in Washington D.C. in January 2003.

Is it foolish or naïve of me to "dream the impossible dream" that the world's peoples may develop a mutual respect for each other and for the diverse groups within their own countries? Is it too much to ask our governments to spend at least as much money on fighting poverty, malnutrition, injustice and environmental degradation as they do on fighting each other and building ever more elaborate systems of defense and attack? Perhaps it is, but unless concerned citizens take a stand on these issues, things will never change. But I get ahead of myself—some of that is covered in the final section!

NEGOTIATION

Finally they chose a round table:
Resurrected relic of regal times
When chivalry reigned supreme.
The world reverberated
With the repercussions
Of this historic moment.

Months passed,
Filled with bitter feuding;
Thrust and parry
Of rivals skilled
In the art of diplomatic warfare:
Charge and counter-charge
Of twisted propaganda.

"All I have is a voice…"
Throughout the world
Protesting voices try to drown
The whine of lead,
The whimper of anguish,
The awful silence of despair.
The world lies bathed
In the red sunset
Which foretells
Impending blackness:

Harry J. Fielding

Death-blood
Of disillusioned soldiers
And uncomprehending peasants
Achieves ironic unity
Impossible in life.

How many pawns
Must be sacrificed
Before the game concludes
In the inevitable stalemate?

"Look, mummy, look—please do!
See what Santa brought me:
An artificial leg, brand new;
Isn't it a beauty!"

And far away in Paris-town
Around a headless table,
Opposing diplomats sit down
To daily spit and squabble.

All I have is a voice,
But not entirely so:
I have eyes blasted and blinded
By battles and bombs,

ABOUT TIME!

And a nose
Sickened by the stench
Of senseless slaughter.
Should I remain
In my accustomed apathy,
My very silence
Condones the atrocities
Of others.

I feel, I mourn, I am:
And all I have is a voice.

Harry J. Fielding

SETTLEMENT
January 27, 1973

So, it's over:
God, what a bloody mess!
Strange,
There's little joy in my heart tonight:
Just a sickening sense of futility.
Peace with honor? Rubbish!
Grovel in your honor!
Brutus, too, was honorable.
Honor? Slaughter, rape and murder,
And all for what?
Stalemate: no move left,
So they call it a mistake,
Clap each other on the back
And apologize.
Hypocritical smiles all round,
And whispered euphemisms:
Facades of friendliness,
But each still hating
The other's guts.
Was it so long ago,
That other futile wish:
"Peace in our time"?

ABOUT TIME!

Let the politicians make war:
Only the people can make peace.
Blessed are the peacemakers:
They who dare to be different.
Damn the politicians!
I won't fight their stinking wars:
What right have I
To decide who should live or die?
In the abstraction of a mechanized age
People destroy people
Without emotion.
God, we need emotion!
Compassion, care and concern:
Let peace begin on earth
And let it begin with me.

Harry J. Fielding

BYGONE DAYS

YESTERDAY
The clarion call
and the ringing response of steel on steel!
Yesterday, the proud-maned stallions
and the crested warriors:
The victor and the vanquished
Locked in mortal conflict!

TODAY
The chivalry, the fair fight,
The blood and sweat of honest battle
Have forever disappeared.

WEEP
for an era gone!
Weep and cower in terror:
For who knows
Whose finger in some near or distant land
Hovers o'er the button marked
DESTRUCTION!

AFTER HIROSHIMA

A flash of silver
In the azure sky:
White vapor trails
At 30,000 feet.
Too high to hear
The shrieking of this bird of prey.
Graceful white arch:
Is this the gateway to God?

On such an evening,
As winter's chill breath
Burns my throat,
Causes my eyes to sparkle
And my brain to race
With unaccustomed clarity of thought—
On such an evening,
I believe in God.

A final flash of silver:
Defiant, daring
Disappearing
Beyond the seen horizon.

Nature, creation, God and I
Merge together

Harry J. Fielding

In the experience of the moment:
A moment so rare,
Indelibly imprinted
In my mind's eye;
To be recaptured
In the tomorrowland of my soul.

The vapor arch remains,
Testimony to human ingenuity
And human foolishness.
Time, the great intangible
Will cause the memory to blur:
Was Hiroshima the end,
Or the beginning of the end?

ABOUT TIME
Washington D.C., January 18, 2003

They came
From many different places
These brave Warriors of Peace.
They came
From every corner of this great land
And from beyond its borders.

They came
By train,
By foot,
By bus
And even in flower-painted minibuses,
Reminiscent of days tho' long ago
Still seem like yesterday.

They came,
Frail and hearty
Old and young
A rainbow collage
Of expectant faces
Half a million strong
To brave the bitter winds and chilling cold
Of this fair city—
To try to change

Harry J. Fielding

The bitter words and chilling policies
Of unfair politicians.
They came
To hear speakers remind them
That the one whose birthday was remembered
Would speak from beyond the grave
To dispel the confines of restricted vision
To remind us all
That for evil to flourish
Good people simply have to say
And do
Nothing!

Its about time
We paid attention to those words
And time
To try another way!

ABOUT TIME!

REFLECTIONS ON DEATH

It is somewhat ironic that I have placed more poems in this section than in any other section of this anthology. I have commented to more than one person, since taking up residence in the United States six years ago, that there appears to be a widespread fear of death and avoidance of dealing with issues related to death in this society. I suppose my viewpoint is colored by the Polynesian attitudes toward death, particularly those of the indigenous Maori people of New Zealand.

The first poem in this section reflects on the death of James K. Baxter, poet, philosopher and social revolutionary. Although a ***pakeha*** (white man) Baxter was loved and respected by all. He made a significant contribution to the cultural and intellectual life of New Zealand.

The next two poems were written while I was at university, the first in my undergraduate days, and the other when I had returned almost 10 years later to complete my MA degree. ***Swan Song*** reflects on the suicide of a fellow-student whom I had seen around the campus, but did not know personally.

Death of My Father was completed just a few moments ago as I came across his photograph and my mind wandered back to his funeral service and from there back to his life as I knew it. No time for honing-you get it just as it came to me, full of roughness and raw emotion!

The fourth poem in this section was actually one of my earlier poems, dating back to the days when I was much more of a bible "literalist" than I am now. I hesitated to include it, but it does reflect part of the intellectual and artistic pathway I have taken. I think that it also, along with the final poem in this section, **Tribute to Columbia**, provides a natural "bridge" to the following section, which brings hope and new life into focus.

ABOUT TIME!

ANNIVERSARY OF DEATH OF JAMES K. BAXTER

Surely,
There among the people that he loved
His spirit rejoiced.
The high-pitched wail of the kuia[1]
Sounded triumphant,
Testimony that the resurrection
Is surely existential in significance.

And did he smile
As he looked upon the well-kept grave?
Did he nod approvingly
That commune and marae[2]
Complemented each other
On this solemn occasion?

Poets and politicians,
Priests, philosophers and people
Came to pay homage
Not just to a man,
But to a way of life.

---

[1] Elderly woman of the Maori people (indigenous Polynesians of New Zealand).
[2] Open space in front of Maori meeting house—symbolizes 'Maoriness'.

Harry J. Fielding

    Kaumatua[3] and kuia
    Joined in the age-old rituals
    For one who had become
    Tangata-whenua[4].

    Poet, philosopher, socialist,
    These he was:
    But foremost, he was human
    And thus a creator and a builder.
    And so,
    He came to this green and
    pleasant land
    And built Jerusalem[5].

---

[3] Tribal elders.
[4] Having land rights and membership rights in local tribe.
[5] Name of commune established by Baxter.

ABOUT TIME!

SWAN SONG

No one was there
To witness the performance.
There was just
The gold-flecked blackness
Stretching before him:
The star-spangled sky
Was his auditorium,
The damp earth, his stage.
This was his finest hour:
The epitome
Of Organic Extinction.
For the first time
He felt free
To be himself.

Yesterday
He had felt like laughing
In the market place.
So he laughed,
Out loud.
The passers-by

Had averted their eyes:
Studiously gazed at the sidewalk;

Harry J. Fielding

"Only a madman laughs at nothing,"
Their expressions said.

Perhaps he was mad:
It was unnatural
To be natural
In a pseudo-world
Of stifled personalities
And carefully suppressed emotions.

He had tried to tell her,
But she hadn't understood.
No one understood;
They wouldn't listen:

They looked at him
In his dirty yellow T shirt
And muttered
Hippie! Junkie!
And averted their eyes.

Now he was laughing
Again.
But this time
There was no audience
To criticize,
Or condemn,
Or even to applaud

ABOUT TIME!

The finest performance
Of his brief career.

There was no restraint,
No suppression,
Just a glorious feeling
Of release.
This was his catharsis,
The merging of his spirit
With the universe.

For several seconds
He was at peace,
Eternally suspended
Between earth and sky.

They found him next morning
And recognized him
As the one who had laughed aloud
In the market place.
They shook their heads,
Pursed their lips,
And averted their eyes.

And **still**
No one understood.

Harry J. Fielding

OBITUARY FOR H.J.F.

Don't grieve me when I die;
Heaven knows
I've caused enough grief while I lived!
Don't eulogize my failings:
Paint them realistically,
For by them
You remember that I was human.
And my strengths:
Remember them also;
They are woven
Into the tapestry of time.
Remember
Not me,
But rather, what I stood for:
Faith, compassion and service.
And where I failed to aspire to these,
Remember
I lacked not vision,
But application.

It's easy to blame society
For one's failings;
Easy to rationalize the individual wrong
In terms of the social influence.

ABOUT TIME!

But the Just Society
Can be created
Only by Just Individuals.

Remember me
Not in floral tributes,
Nor in annual notices in the daily papers:
Remember me
By the quality of YOUR contributions
To the Just Society.

Harry J. Fielding

DEATH OF MY FATHER
October 4, 2002

He slunk away
Like a disturbed dingo
Scared in scavenging scraps
To feed its young.

He left
As he had done so many times before
Without a fond farewell
Or even a gruff and throaty grunt.

He left
A closet full of old clothes,
Some dirty and ragged
Symbolic of his early fatherhood.

When did he break the booze?
I don't recall,
But it was sometime after I quit
My cowardly cowering under the bedcovers,
Hiding in horror at the raised voices
While listening to the sound of vomit
Sloshing in the toilet bowl.

ABOUT TIME!

He never said "I love you"
To us kids
And seldom to his wife,
Yet beneath that gruff exterior
Was a sometimes-soft streak:
He would give you the shirt off his back
If you needed it.

And now he stares unseeing from his wooden box,
Not able to greet or scorn his many guests,
Some expected, but quite a few surprising by their presence.
Would that I could see him raise his missing finger
One last time,
In gesture of defiance and endearment
At we who gather in respect and love
And at death's dark angel hovering near.

Harry J. Fielding

THE GARDEN

The hour was come.
He sighed; he glanced around
In sorrow; the senseless ground
Beneath him, seemed to groan;
Intense anguish filled his every bone:
His heart was numb.

How still the air!
He paused; his thirsty sight
Drank deep the glories of the night;
The tears ran, unheeded, down his cheek;
The silence all about him seemed to speak!
He strained to hear.

His brow was wet.
His perspiration was unreal;
The dark could not conceal
This fact: his brow was oozing red
From every pore—perspiring blood, instead
Of ordinary sweat.

He raised his face.
Distant voices pierced the night,
Came closer; in the flickering light
One whom he knew well, ran

ABOUT TIME!

To kiss him; betrayed the sorrowing man
By this embrace.

His face was sad.
Worse was yet to come:
His friends disloyal—some
Would renounce him. He smiled then:
Humankind could live again
And he was glad.

Harry J. Fielding

TRIBUTE TO COLUMBIA
Reflections on of February 1, 2003

Space:
The Last Frontier
Or so they say.
Well,
So it proved
For these brave souls
The Magnificent Seven
Riding into their final sunset:
Rendezvous with death.
History will remember them
As scientists
Seeking knowledge and advancement
For the World.

Anderson, Brown, Chawla, Clark,
Husband, McCool and Ramon:
Names not well known
A few days ago
Just another routine mission
Into the Last Frontier.

Last, perhaps,
But hardly final,
For the memory will endure

ABOUT TIME!

Through human history.

"Life continues in lots of places,
And life is a magical thing."
So said Laurel Clark
As she watched the transformation
Of worm into moth—
Of death into life.

And so
Framed by the dark canopy
Of that Last Frontier
Seven new stars
Shine brightly—
And life continues.

Harry J. Fielding

NEW LIFE

Okay, I admit it-I have just a small streak of existentialism in my beliefs. You could also throw in some process thought and a fairly large dollop of Christian humanism. So I'm a crazy mixed up Kiwi!

I firmly believe that orthodox Christian beliefs are no longer adequate to address the worldview of the 21st century. Yet I still give a little room for the mystery of the divine. I won't get too technical here, or this will end up being a book on theology. Suffice to say that I believe we are all connected together and indeed are connected with all living matter, vegetable and animal. I like to express it as being immersed in the "sea of the divine" in which everything exists.

In this sense I do not believe in "the" incarnation in the traditional Christian sense. I do, however, firmly believe in the *principle* of incarnation, which is enacted "every day in every way." And before hundreds of God-fearing Christians take my book and throw it into the fire, or peevishly hit the "delete"

Harry J. Fielding

button on their computer keyboards, let me remind you that Christianity by no means holds exclusive rights to beliefs about "God becoming human" (sorry, but my MA degree was in cultural anthropology).

    The poems in this section stress the importance of existence here and now (hence my reference to myself as an "existentialist") and in the conquering power of love.

    End of sermon!

INCARNATION

Beauty is truth, truth beauty, that is all
Ye know on earth and all ye need to know. **John Keats**

For a moment,
A lifetime of intensity
Their lives were one:
She was a part of him
And he of her;
Together
They formed a perfect whole.

They sat there, mute,
Under the darkened sky.
The fullness of their communion
Precluded words:
The ultimate empathy was theirs.

It had been this way
From the dawn of creation.
They had been together
For all eternity.
They were no more,
No less,
Than this:
They were

Harry J. Fielding

What they were.

Time has no limitations
For those
Who transcend the finite
And dwell in the realms of Spirit.

"Goodnight," she said.
They parted;
Went their separate ways,
Confident
That the transient eternity
Which was theirs
Would be renewed.
Incarnation
Depends upon
Finite limitations:
"Goodnight," he said.

DAYBREAK

We shared together, you and I,
That unforgettable moment,
While the gray mist
Stubbornly sought to obscure our vision.
Clammy fingers
Reached inevitably upward,
Seeking to engulf, to smother
The Source of Life.
Burned fingers - helpless:
Drawn, like a moth, to destruction
In the flame;
Recoiling in pain:
Opening,
To allow the Birth of Life.

With the Dawn
Our spirits awakened:
We became
In that instant of comprehension
Co-creators
Of a New Day!

Harry J. Fielding

REGENERATION

The enrichment of love,
Nourishing drought-struck lives;
New relationships,
New attitudes,
New view of self.
A vision glimpsed,
Partially shared,
Not yet understood:
My personhood is incomplete
Without your love:
Yours, without mine.
Reciprocation, involvement, honesty,
Turn my wasteland
Into a garden of self-fulfillment:
In your presence
The dark and bitter waste of winter
Surrenders to the sweet success of spring.

ABOUT TIME!

IN LIGHTER VEIN

Just to prove that impassioned preachers/social activists can sometimes "lighten up" a little, I've included a few somewhat frivolous offerings. **Lake Wanaka,** is in the South Island of New Zealand. This is purely and simply a nature poem and is probably the oldest in the anthology. I have been fortunate to travel in many beautiful places in the world and I have to say (of course as a purely unbiased Kiwi) that Lake Wanaka in Autumn ranks among the very best of the scenic places I have viewed.

The *haiku* were written during my first year of teaching, my previous occupation in "another life." They follow the traditional Japanese pattern of first and last lines with 5 syllables each, with a middle line of 7 syllables.

The **Convenient Country Churchyard,** is of course a lighthearted parody of Gray's poem, "An Elegy Written in a Country Churchyard." I make no apology for including it—I had a lot of fun writing it!

Harry J. Fielding

The Journey, whilst basically lighthearted in style, hints at some deeper questions and thus provides transition into the final section. It was written many years ago on an airplane traveling from Auckland, New Zealand to Sydney, Australia.

SUNSET ON LAKE WANAKA

Blue sky, barren hills,
On a mountain range, some snow,
Golden poplars, bellbird trills,
Gentle autumn breezes blow.

Bright sun, noonday heat,
Gentle waves lap on the shore,
Artists painting; at their feet,
Reflected, scenes of nature's law.

Cool wind, evening nigh,
Sun sinking in the west,
People gazing, orange sky,
Nature settling down to rest.

Red now, purple, blue,
Snowcapped mountains clear and stark:
Violet, crimson, every hue,
Quickly fading; all is dark.

Harry J. Fielding

HAIKU

Autumn Poplars
Dressed in gold costume
They dance in joyous fashion
On their thick carpet

The Cricket
He steps carefully
To avoid the six-legged
Cheerful black nuisance

Summer School
Part 1
Wait! Wait! Now at last
The whole class gets the message:
Silence is golden!

Part 2
Attentive heads bent
Noses trying to remove
Freshly formed writing

ABOUT TIME!

NO CONVENIENT COUNTRY CHURCHYARD

The late night movie plays its final scene,
The mewing cat outside is now at peace,
The clock shows witching hour has passed unseen,
The pen must soon its weary movements cease.

Soon fades the light bulb burning in my room,
Then must the air be still, for I must sleep,
Then nothing must disturb the solemn gloom,
Save drowsy snorings from my lips may leap.

Oft did the pages to the pen's nib yield,
Each pearl of wisdom there forever writ,
The pen, than sword more difficult to wield,
Records the poet's fast declining wit.

Let not ambition make this poem too long,
For brevity's indeed the soul of wit,
And grandeur may be well disdained as wrong,
When short and simple words the mood best fit.

Here at the foot of my inviting bed
I pen these words for you to understand,

Harry J. Fielding

Upon the pillow I fain would rest my head,
For Morpheus seeks to lead me by the hand.

How true it is of ev'ry good desire,
That unseen factors cause resolve to crack,
Now first one foot, now two, are in the mire,
Light footsteps sink: there is no turning back.

The Epitaph:
Here rests my head upon my innersprung,
I dream of fortune, fame, and worlds to gain,
And 'tho my praises may be never sung,
I have known great joy as well as pain.
I do not seek my merits to display,
My frailties are many, as you can see,
Now Morpheus will no longer keep at bay,
I leave the world to darkness, and to thee.

ABOUT TIME!

THE JOURNEY

The oppression
That settled like an epidemic
Over the town
Is ebbing—waning as the day wanes.
The incessant throbbing in my head will drive me mad!

Throb! Throb! Throb…
For God's sake, move that time faster:
You're omnipotent, aren't you?

Throb! Throb! Crackle…
"Passengers leaving on flight 1725…"
Throb! Throb! Throb!
What if I should fly forever, God:
Would I reach eternity?
Huh, God, would I?

Like a crab scuttling backward,
I regress: Back, back;
Glory, what a sunset!
Throb! Throb! Throb!
You're omnipotent, aren't you?

Harry J. Fielding

ABOUT TIME!

JUSTICE OR JUST US?

The title says it all. As a Christian minister I have been privileged to work in the South Pacific and my current assignment is in the Caribbean, although I live in Orlando, Florida. I get to visit Haiti 3 or 4 times per year. Haiti is the poorest country, economically, in the western hemisphere, with an average life expectancy in the low to mid-fifties. There are many places in Haiti without electricity or running water. Hills have been stripped bare of vegetation to provide fuel for cooking fires. These images came strongly into my mind one evening as I was skiing in Colorado. Although I am not rich by western standards, in the eyes of the Haitians I am a wealthy man. Perhaps you are rich also, without knowing it. If you own your own car and are living in your own home, you are in the top 5% of the world's population from an economic standpoint.

The above factors provided the stimulus for me to write ***Perspectives,*** a poem which gained me third place award in a competition run by the ***International Library of Poetry*** in 2002. I constantly struggle with guilt feelings about the resources I squander every day, yet I also firmly believe, there is "enough and to spare." I believe that if enough of us seriously work at overcoming the social and economic problems that beset us on every side, we can truly live in Peace.

We are children of the future. Our actions and attitudes create the kind of future that will be. I do not believe that God sits up in the sky like some magic genie, waiting to wave a wand and make the future suddenly materialize. If there is to be a World of Peace it will be because you and I make conscious efforts to build bridges rather than barriers. That is why my final poem, **The Proposal,** is directed at you, the reader. It was inspired by Tennyson's account of the mythical voyage in his poem **Ulysses.** Come with me on our own journey of discovery and let us together build a New Way, Together.

PERSPECTIVES

Protruding rugged rocks:
Endless panorama of crystals
Alive with purple, blue and red.
The crimson orb above
Sends its last gasping breath
To touch its infant offspring far below.
Picture of postcard perfection
Caressed by the soft whisper of skis:
Playground of the RICH.

Protruding ragged roofs:
Enveloping blanket of blackness;
Perpetual panorama of pain
Lacking the presence of light
And the brightness of hope.
Firelight flickering red, blue and purple
Over bare hillsides, denuded of trees
Slain to provide charcoal for cooking fires:
Habitation of the POOR.

Harry J. Fielding

A SEARCH FOR MEANING

I sought for meaning in galactic space
Where ephemeral orbs offered transient hope
Within the dark illusion of their brightness,
And meaning was not there.

I sought for meaning in a world
Where futile wars were raging
And human blindness rationalized
Human killing human,
And meaning was not there.

I sought for meaning in the world of science
Where Darwinian theories
Told me how, not why I am,
And meaning was not there.

I sought for meaning
Deep within my cynic's heart,
And found a spark of Love Divine,
And THIS was meaning!

CHILD OF THE FUTURE

So many try to say Not Now
So many have forgotten how
To say I Am and would be
Lost, if they could, in history. W.H. Auden

To take each moment
And live it utterly;
To immerse yourself
In the excitement of a changing world:
This is your calling.

To love and be loved,
To accept without reserve;
To forgive willingly
Because you have been forgiven:
This is your hope.

To say I AM;
To give Life
To the experience of the moment;
To take the present
And mold a worthwhile future:
This is your destiny.

Harry J. Fielding

Child of the Future,
The present needs you
Desperately.
So many die unloved
And unloving;
So many lonely souls
Cry out for comfort:
THERE IS NO OTHER TIME, BUT NOW!

THE PROPOSAL

Come, my friend,
For I am grown weary
Of this life.
When I was young,
I thought that I could change the world;
Now my experience-blasted soul
Sees through its burnished window
More clearly.

I see you for what you are:
An idealist—an optimist
Who still retains
A measure of blind faith
In humankind.

Come then, with me:
Let us build a New Way!
There must be kindred souls
Who dare to seek another world!

My soul
Awaits a revelation:
From within,
Or from without,
I cannot tell.

Harry J. Fielding

Once, I believed
In the future;
Now,
I believe in myself,
And in you.
My cynicism
Thrives upon
Your passionate intensity.

Come then,
Let us build a new life
Together!

TWO ESSAYS

The two essays that follow have not previously been published, although certain sections have been presented at theology colloquies and used in sermons. They are written for the 'average' reader, rather than as scholarly presentations.

The first, while dealing with the broad subject of how we form beliefs and values, is also inextricably related to issues of peace and justice. I make no apologies for that—the lens through which I view my world sees peace and justice issues in almost every sphere of existence.

The second essay obviously stems from my vocation as a Christian minister. It focuses upon the life and ministry of Jesus Christ as a model for promoting unity in the world. I do not mean to imply that Jesus is the only model possible: I personally find much inspiration in the lives of influential figures from many of the world's great religions. But I am more familiar with the life of Jesus Christ and it is out of this familiarity that I share my ideas.

Harry J. Fielding

I BELIEVE

How I Believe

A while ago my television showed me news of a space shuttle charting a three dimensional map of the world. It also showed me the effects of tornadoes in Georgia, USA and hostages returning home from a hijacked plane in London, England. Recently I listened on the radio to a man who claimed to be a reincarnated saint from the 19th century. In his country of Tibet the concept of 'self-esteem' was totally incomprehensible. In his religious worldview a person could only truly be a 'self' in relationship to other persons or 'selves'. Therefore one could only truly have esteem in terms of social relationships. 'Self-esteem', for this man was simply nonsense.

These few examples illustrate the complexity of the world in which we live. It is a world which has a great deal of interconnectedness. The contemporary world has sometimes been referred to as a 'global village' because of the relative ease of communication and travel. Perhaps, 'global

ABOUT TIME!

city' might be a more accurate description, for rural villages and farms are being swallowed at an alarming rate by the prolific growth of urban cities worldwide. I expect that in my children's lifetime, space travel will become a common occurrence, readily available to those who have the money to pay for it. By that time we will doubtless have a world 'currency'—not actual notes and coins you understand, but stored credit in the next stage of electronic banking.

The changing face of the world and technology in the last century has also brought profound changes to the religious life of the world. And it is not only the character of religious life that has undergone change, but also the methods used to study religion. The 'modern' and 'post-modern' approaches to the study of theology and religion which have developed in the last century or so, had their roots in the last few decades of the 18th century, in the period known as the 'European Enlightenment'. This essay is not the place for a detailed examination of those approaches; suffice to say that the impact today of science and technology on the social sciences (including religion) has been profound.

Harry J. Fielding

For the modern student of religion ***how*** we believe is just as important as ***what*** we believe. The development of the global city has meant that there has been a growing exposure, in most countries around the world, to cultural practices and religious belief systems that may appear to be very different from one's own culture and religion. In the past, people generally found it easier to dismiss these practices and beliefs as heretical, ignorant, or just plain 'wrong'. This included differences ***within*** faith traditions (for example, Roman Catholic beliefs as opposed to Protestant beliefs, within Christianity) as well as ***between*** them (for example, between Islam and Judaism). Cross cultural studies in recent times have focused not only upon the content of those differences, but also upon the cultural and historic factors which have led to the formation of those beliefs in the first place. Some studies have sought to identify central principles that are common to religious life in general.

I believe that developing understanding and cooperation between the major religious faiths of the world is one of the most critical issues

ABOUT TIME!

facing us in the 21st century. In the name of religion terrorists find justification for their actions. In the name of religion wars between countries and within countries (so called 'civil wars', but most times they are anything but civil!) have been and continue to be waged. In the name of religion and freedom politicians find justification in bombing cities and towns where hundreds of thousands of innocent victims are killed. In the name of the major world religions, I believe that we must build bridges to connect us rather than barriers to keep us apart.

In April, 2000 I attended a World Conference of the ***Community of Christ*** where delegates representing more than 40 countries were assembled. Although it was a Christian conference, many of the delegates came from countries where Christianity is a minority religion. In his keynote sermon, the president of the ***Community of Christ,*** W. Grant McMurray stated:

> ***Our commitment should be to coexist in love and peace, to be willing to learn from one another, to share our common witness to the extent we can,***

and to be respectful of those traditions that shape the souls of billions of people around the world. To do so is not to divest ourselves of the zeal inherent in our own witness. It is to embrace the fundamental principle of the Christian, which is love of God and love of neighbor...Let us be reconciled to brothers and sisters of other faiths and religions by authentically expressing our witness and being respectful of theirs.

To which I simply add, "Amen."

If we are to build bridges of understanding and cooperation, it is important that we understand at least the basics of what 'religion' is and how we form religious beliefs and values. Too often religious adherents do not 'think through' their religious beliefs - they simply accept them as a factual representation of the way the world 'is'. If we are to have any hope of developing religious tolerance and understanding, and especially if we wish to foster religious diversity in our world, we must not only understand, but also be willing to accept, that there are many different ways of looking at the 'world'.

The concept of 'religion' as a noun that describes a specific set of beliefs and practices, particularly with a supernatural dimension, is quite a recent phenomenon which has arisen in the West. Throughout most of human history people have not thought of themselves as belonging to or 'having' a 'religion'. Even today, the Chinese do not have a word for 'religion' in the sense of a set of beliefs and practices to be embraced. W. Cantwell Smith, in his important book, ***The Meaning and End of Religion,*** has challenged his readers to stop thinking of religion as a 'thing', made up of beliefs, rituals, scriptures, moral codes, etc. These are human products arising from the religious dimension of human existence. They are created, modified and discarded as circumstances change. Smith called these the 'cumulative tradition' of each religious path and he emphasized the importance of asking how and why these cumulative traditions evolved in the first place.

What Smith called a cumulative tradition is roughly comparable to what anthropologists and sociologists would describe today as a 'culture'. Following E.B. Tylor, culture could be described as a complex whole that includes knowledge, belief, art, morals, law, customs and social conventions. Religion is not singled out as a separate component, because it is a dimension of the complex whole. Religion and culture are so interwoven that they are not separable: neither can exist without the other, or as Paul Tillich has expressed it, they 'interpenetrate' each other. The 'religious element' in culture, according to Tillich, is "the substance or ground from which culture lives. It is the element of ultimacy which culture lacks in itself but to which it points."[1] This is a somewhat difficult idea for modern humans to grasp, particularly in countries such as the USA where differences between 'state' and 'religion' are enshrined in the political Constitution. However, there is a rapidly escalating trend in Western society to recapture a wholistic or 'relational' approach to life. There would be very few school students today who would not be aware of the concept of 'ecosystems' and cause and effect relationships between all of the various aspects of physical

---

[1] Paul Tillich, *Systematic Theology,* Vol 111, p.101

existence. That same approach is finding growing expression in religious circles. For example, this constitutes much of the approach taken by theologian Sally McFague in her model of the universe as 'God's body'.

Mc Fague presents a concept which is critical for us to embrace in this day and age where human actions are unquestionably threatening the continued long-term existence of the world in which we live and of which we are a part. In her book, **Super, Natural Christians,** McFague suggests that Christians are called to love nature in exactly the same way that we are called to love God and our fellow humans. Until we recognize that all of God's creation is of equal worth, we are doomed to mistreat and exploit nature. According to McFague, we need to treat nature as a **subject** rather than as an object. The Genesis view of creation as being "good" does not mean that creation is "good for humans" or even "good for God"; creation is just "good in its own right." I believe that our attitude toward nature is very much part of the wholistic picture of peace that Christians are called to embrace.

What does all this have to do with a Jewish carpenter who lived more than 2000 years ago, before the time of motor cars, television, and fast food stores with a big yellow M in front? The answer is simple. People in Jesus' day were much like people today—there were rich and poor, righteous and self-righteous, insiders and outsiders, and ethnic and religious minorities who faced prejudice and discrimination just as they do today. Jesus was intensely concerned with creating a just society, where all were of equal worth. He called this society the 'kingdom of God'. It is unfortunate that those who came after him have often misunderstood his message, or have sometimes distorted it to suit their own purposes.

The principles which Jesus taught and lived are relatively easy to understand—they are much more difficult to apply, but unless we begin to do so, we may well destroy the world in which we live. In the 20th century, for the first time in the history of the world, humankind developed the technology to literally destroy the world. Furthermore, it may not take a willful act of purpose for such destruction to occur. Environmentalists, scientists, and many others point to developing trends in contemporary society which are slowly but surely destroying the fragile ecosystem of the planet that we call 'home'. Optimists predict that if present trends continue, our world will be able to support life as we know it for just a few thousand more years. Pessimists look at the mounting evidence pointing toward an impending global catastrophe and claim that we may only have a few hundred years.

The Wrong End of the Telescope!

Not too many of us own a telescope. Some of us have been fortunate at some time or another to look through a powerful telescope or to have been in an observatory and to see the wondrous image of the stars magnified hundreds or even thousands of times. What a different world we see when we use a powerful telescope properly! Who could have imagined that the invention of the telescope by Galileo Galilei almost 400 years ago, would have started us upon a journey that has literally revolutionized the way we understand the world in which we live.

Galileo, using his newly invented telescope, verified what Nicolas Copernicus had said in 1530: the sun does not revolve around the earth, but rather the reverse is true. Any elementary school pupil will today be able to verify that truth, but in the 16th and 17th centuries the earth was regarded as the center of the universe. Galileo was summoned to appear before the Inquisition of the church on charges of heresy. Under threat of death he was forced to 'recant' or withdraw his claims. Church officials were upset that Galileo's views appeared to contradict the Bible and to threaten the authority of the church.

The story of Galileo demonstrates that each of us looks at the world in a certain way, which is influenced by the time and circumstances in which we live. We call this our 'worldview'. In a very real sense each of us 'creates' the world in which we live. Of course we cannot claim credit for creating the sun or the earth, nor for constructing the basic biological 'building blocks' of life. But we do create and alter the environment in which we live. The houses we live in, the clothes we wear, the cars we drive are all made by humans. The jobs we do, the entertainment and recreation in which we participate are all part of a culture that is humanly constructed. In this sense humans are world-builders.

Beneath the surface of the physical world that we have constructed, lies an invisible world of values and beliefs. This is a world in which we interpret our experiences and relationships. In this 'deep world' we try to discover meaning and purpose in and for existence. This world includes those concepts that we call 'religious', including our understanding of God. Properly speaking, this 'deep world' is not a separate world at all: it is part of the 'real world' of physical 'things'. It is as much humanly created as is the physical world described above. Actually, the 'real world' is not an independent external 'reality'; it is a relative world that only takes on meaning as we interact with it.

Sociologist Clifford Geertz once described humans as animals suspended in webs of significance that we ourselves have spun. To extend Geertz's metaphor, we should recognize that as we move around our web of significance (or 'shift our position', if you will), we see our world from a different vantage point, and thus develop new understandings. Furthermore, we are continually adding 'new strands' to our webs as we encounter new experiences and share in the experiences of others. And as our individual webs (worlds) come in contact with and intersect the worlds of others, we are able to explore a little (and perhaps come to some understanding of) worldviews that are different from our own.

Perhaps the above will be easier to understand if we know that the English word 'world' comes from the old German language and is composed of two parts—***wer*** (man) and ***ald*** (age). Literally speaking, 'world' refers to the age or context in which we live. We can understand this in such expressions as "she lives in a different world from me", or such references as the 'world of politics' or the 'art world'. Once we understand that we each interpret the world through our own experiences, values and beliefs, it makes it a little easier to accept that another person's world is as real and right for them as mine is for me. In today's global city this is an ***essential*** concept to grasp.

In light of the above, it goes without saying that the viewpoints and opinions expressed in this essay are my own. They reflect my understandings and experiences at this point in my life. If I had written this essay 20 years ago, I suspect that it would have been markedly different from that which is now presented. Similarly, if I were to project myself 10 or 20 years into the future, I would expect that my viewpoints and understandings would be expressed differently. When we cease to learn, we cease to grow.

In the formation of our beliefs, both at an individual level and at a wider group level, language plays a crucial part. We use words to try and express our understandings, but words are always, at best, inadequate and very often counter-productive. Words, whether spoken or written, are *symbols*, that represent (*re*-present) ideas, understandings and concepts. We each understand and interpret the 'reality' of our world through the medium of language. Bruce Gregory expresses this well:

> *Language tells us what the world is made of, not because language*

> *somehow accurately captures a world independent of language, but because it is the heart of our way of dealing with the world. When we create a new way of talking about the world, we virtually create a new world...Explanations, no matter how wonderful, are stories about how we got from where we were to where we are.[2]*

In terms of religious beliefs, much of the time, the language takes the form of tradition stories or mythological narratives. These are rich in meaning and often express in symbolic and metaphorical form the cherished values and beliefs of the society of which they are a part. Very often they are not intended to be taken literally. They are not stories of historical fact. Yet though they may be imaginative stories, they express ultimate convictions of the people or culture from which they arise. In this sense they are 'true' stories. Only for those who stand outside that culture do the myths appear to be false or nonsensical. At a very simple level, Christians recognize this. For example, the vast majority of Christians

---

[2] Bruce Gregory, *Inventing Reality: Physics as Language,* John Wiley & Sons, 1988, p.198

ABOUT TIME!

would acknowledge that the parables that Jesus used did not depict historically factual events. They were, for the most part, what we would call today, 'sermon illustrations'. Yet that does not stop them from being effective tools to convey the 'truths' that Jesus was trying to teach. What is somewhat difficult, however, for many Christians to accept, is the claim made by many contemporary theologians and bible students, that many of the stories *about* Jesus in the New Testament should be regarded as myths—i.e. they teach convictions and beliefs that the early Christian community held as 'truths', but the stories themselves were not necessarily 'true' in the sense of being historically accurate. The 'truth' lies not in the stories themselves, but rather in the underlying conviction that here was someone special, one who in his life and ministry and even in the nature of his death, somehow had captured and expressed the 'divine truth' that pervades our entire universe, but of which most of us are only dimly aware.

To understand how the life of Jesus can be a model for today's world, we will need to trace some of the developments and changes from his time to ours. Physical or material changes are relatively easy to recognize; what will be more difficult and probably upsetting for many people to realize are the changes that have happened in our religious worldview. All of the major world religions have undergone profound changes, but probably none more so than Christianity which began as a Jewish sect and spread beyond the geographic and theological boundaries of Judaism to become a world religion in its own right.

The Jewish worldview in the time of Jesus was markedly different from the way we view the world today. It was even quite different from the prevailing worldview in the time of Galileo. The worldview in Jesus' time was intimately associated with the world of spirit. Yet although the Hebrews distinguished between 'this-world' and the world of spirit, the spirit-world was not thought to be literally located 'someplace else.' The spirit world was regarded as a particular dimension of this world, and the presence of God pervaded the entire universe.

In the centuries after Jesus, Christianity began to spread, and it was particularly the influence of Greek mythology and belief and also that of Zoroastrian religious thought from Persia, that developed what is referred to as 'dualism' in Christian thought. Dualism proposes a strict separation of the world of spirit and establishes it as the 'other-world' as opposed to 'this-world' of time and space. In early Christian thought, heaven was regarded as a literal place located in the sky. There was thought to be a hard shell above the earth and the stars were the windows to heaven. Hell was also regarded as a literal place 'beneath' the earth, no doubt influenced by Greek mythology about the 'underworld'. In this worldview, the concept of a God who 'came down' from heaven and took on human form, made perfectly good sense. It was hardly a unique concept; many religions had myths and tradition stories about gods who took on human form and also about 'demi- gods' who had both divine and human attributes, but it was given a new twist in the Christian doctrine of the 'incarnation' which proposed that Jesus Christ was fully God and fully human. It is important to realize that, as far as we can ascertain, this doctrine was not taught by Jesus himself, but emerged after his death.

Harry J. Fielding

In the 13th century, the epic voyages of Marco Polo and other explorers to far-away places challenged the widespread belief that the earth was flat. Yet even up to the time of Copernicus, this was what many people believed. The theories of Copernicus, and Galileo's subsequent substantiation of these with his telescope, began to undermine this widespread belief. They also challenged the authority of the church, which had established itself as the intermediary between heaven and earth. Even before Galileo, the Dominican friar Giordano Bruno had come to the conclusion that a dual worldview of the cosmos was no longer tenable. Bruno began by merging together the earth and the heavens and in a later, more radical development, merged God and the universe together. The universe itself, in Bruno's view, was the unique incarnation (physical expression) of God.

The scientific view that developed after the time of Galileo has largely resulted in the demise of the dual world view. The 20th century saw the emergence of the secular worldview in which there is only this-world of time and space. The mystical other-world has been incorporated into this-world, and most of the orthodox beliefs of the Christian church have been under increasing attack. Yet many Christians refuse to let go or modify their beliefs, not recognizing that they arose in another time and place and grew out of mythology and symbolism associated with a worldview that is largely irrelevant today.

In the second half of the twentieth century there was a significant decline in attendances at mainline Christian denominations, both Protestant and Catholic. There was a marked growth in the numbers of people attending Christian charismatic groups, sometimes referred to as the 'Pentecostal movement.' There was also a plethora of so-called 'new-age' groups and alternative religious groups which sprang forth. Studies among 'Generation X' college students showed that a majority were seeking significant religious experiences, but that traditional (or 'orthodox') religion did not satisfy their requirements.

At the same time that mainline Christianity was declining, and charismatic groups were growing, there was a renewed interest in 'Jesus studies'. The quest for the historical Jesus which had emerged at the beginning of the 20th

century, had faltered and all but died in the aftermath of two world wars and a severe worldwide economic depression. By the middle of the 20th century there was a widespread religious cynicism within western society, leading to what became known as the 'death of God' viewpoint, followed by the 'demythologizing' theologies which came to their peak in the 1960s and 1970s. These theologies called into question traditional orthodox doctrines about Jesus Christ, such doctrines as the virgin birth, the incarnation of God in Christ and the literal bodily resurrection of Jesus Christ.

Even as orthodox Christian beliefs about God and Jesus Christ were under attack in the first world countries, there was a second-pronged attack from the third world. This approach, known as 'liberation theology' was as much upon the institution of the church as upon orthodox doctrine. Faced with problems of starvation, overpopulation, economic exploitation, overwhelming illiteracy and systemic political oppression, voices from the third world protested that the picture of Jesus and God presented by orthodox mainline churches not only failed to address the needs of the third world, but at many points actually promoted and supported the injustices that were taking place. These voices were joined by others, both in the third world and in the first world, clamoring for the attention of the church to be directed toward such issues as gender discrimination, racial and ethnic prejudice, homophobia, ecological issues, and religious and cultural pluralism. To sum up, the evidence points to the prevalence of a widespread spiritual hunger in the last part of the 20th century, which orthodox mainline Christian religion had failed to satisfy, despite the reaction of the orthodox church to shore up the bulwarks of orthodox doctrine. A relatively recent trend known as 'radical orthodoxy' has sought to recapture the 'golden age' of the thirteenth century, but this brand of 'restorationism' appears to raise more problems than solutions.

Conclusion:

We live in a time of rapid change. Not only that, but as sociologists have pointed out, the *rate* of change itself is continually increasing. Such times are always stressful. Religious change also brings with it a high degree of stress. The twentieth century evidenced an unprecedented attack upon traditional religious worldviews and values. Science and modern knowledge have been highly disruptive to traditional western Christianity, causing a ferment of religious ideas and experimentation, as people have sought to satisfy their spiritual yearnings. Many have sought to insulate themselves from the process of modernization and have sought refuge in clinging to the tattered remnants of the old order so that they might protect themselves from the threats and challenges of the new.

The impact of new technologies has been impressive. It hardly seems possible that at the beginning of the twentieth century we did not enjoy such 'luxuries' as air conditioning and refrigeration. Many people were still without electricity and washing machines. Computers were a distant dream. Yet even more impressive than the array of new gadgets that adorn most western households, has been the profound effect of the new ways of thinking that are foundational to those technologies. The 'scientific method' utilizes a procedure for arriving at the 'truth' which in many respects is the exact opposite of the procedure which has been traditionally employed and taught in religious communities. Nothing is sacrosanct and everything is subject to skeptical scrutiny. Whatever survives this rigorous process is kept (at least for the present) and whatever fails the test is ruthlessly discarded, no matter how widely it has been taught and accepted in the past and no matter how great the authority that either introduced it or followed it. In modern scientific thought it is continually emphasized that all theories are humanly created and therefore provisional. Sooner or later they will be either replaced or reformulated. Scientific knowledge is built upon a firm foundation of doubt, and, ideally at least, the scientific community is one in which its members rejoice when new knowledge replaces that which has been previously regarded as 'true'.

The development of scientific approaches to knowledge has had profound effects upon religious thought in the twentieth century. Religious change is inevitable when cultural and scientific changes occur. Even those who seek to slavishly follow the old traditions and to deny and resist the changes which are happening around them, cannot change the fact that even if the beliefs and practices and the religious language to which they cling remain intact, their significance is often profoundly altered by changes in the surrounding culture. Religious change is forced by cultural change, and the tendency for such forced and involuntary change is to most often degrade faith into superstition. In this respect, as Don Cupitt notes, the efforts of contemporary theologians to rescue Christianity from becoming a religion of superstition has often been both misunderstood and unappreciated by many Christians:

> *The theologians' efforts to demythologise Christianity in order to prevent it from decaying into superstition have so far had little lasting success because most people have instinctively felt that the heart of the matter lies in the myth, understood literally, and have persisted in thinking so even while the authority of the myth has been visibly deteriorating all around them...Doctrine, supernatural belief, may be tenaciously maintained, but it becomes psychologised, privatised, a matter of one's secret identity and no longer effectively*

> *connected with the way one behaves in one's real social and economic life. Like a coat of arms, such belief may anchor us reassuringly in the past; but it is of little use in the present.[3]*

What then, are we to make of Jesus in the 21st century? How is his life relevant to the problems and opportunities of the contemporary world? I believe that if Jesus is to have enduring value in this secular age, we must strip away the mythologies and misunderstandings that have developed around him over the centuries and see what it is about his life that can inspire and instruct us today.

We must see 'beyond the horizon' of our limited understanding. To do so, we must exercise 'eyes of faith' that are not limited by the conditioning that we have inherited from those who shaped their faith stories from worldviews that were significantly (even radically) different from our own. Yet we must understand the depth of their conviction that here was a 'savior' who had come to rescue humankind from the predicament of self-

---
[3] Don Cupitt, *The Sea of Faith*, pp 10,11

centeredness and exclusivity that was destroying the integrity of the world. Surely the message of peace and justice for all, of the reality of the divine in the midst of human existence and the vision of a world where all humans and indeed every aspect of existence is bound together in divine relationship, is a message which is particularly relevant and crucially important in the era of the global city. Jesus called this vision the 'kingdom of God', or as some translations (and I myself) prefer, the 'rule of God.'

There are some mighty rivers in the USA, the country where I am now living and in Australia (My wife's native country). These, however, pale by comparison with some of the vast expanses of water found in South America. The Amazon river, for example, seems to stretch for ever—it is barely possible to see one bank from the other. At the headwaters of the Amazon, two huge rivers join together. One is the Negro river which comes down out of Columbia and Venezuela. As the name suggests, the waters of the Negro river are almost pitch black. The other river is the Solomon which comes down from the mountains of Peru and Ecuador. The waters of this river, like the gold from Solomon's mines, are bright yellow in color. When these two rivers join, to form the Amazon, a remarkable thing happens. Instead of mixing together to form a dirty brown color, for almost 20 miles the two rivers race along side by side, each sharing the same channel, each pursuing the same course, but each maintaining its own identity. Perhaps here is a model for us as we seek to develop an attitude of respectfulness toward other religious traditions that exist side by side with our own.

If Jesus Christ is to be a 'savior' for those who dwell in the global city of today and tomorrow, it will be cause we see in his life an appropriate and relevant model for human existence. If he is to be our 'redeemer' it will be because his life challenges us to take responsibility for our individual lives and for the emerging global city in which we dwell. If Jesus is to be perceived as 'messiah', it will be because his life delivers us from the slavery and idolatory of beliefs and values that are exclusive, rather than inclusive, that cause division rather than creating harmony.

Following Galileo, we can seek for an expanded view of our world. Or we can refuse to do so, and in effect look down the wrong end of the telescope and see our world shrinking. Christians today must face the realities of living in a secular world and reinterpret their beliefs to meet the challenges that this-world presents, always recognizing that the 'truth' of our beliefs is relative and limited by the worldview that each of us holds. As we seek to 'bear testimony' in today's world, we should recognize that *how* we testify is at least as important as *what* we testify of. It is in building gospel-centered relationships that we are most effective as witnesses. We do need to identify our 'core values' and beliefs, but perhaps even more important than the 'propositional approach' of teaching a set of beliefs is the relational approach of demonstrating those beliefs in action.

In today's global city it is essential that we dialogue with each other as Christians and with those who embrace other religious traditions, seeking always to understand and become enriched by the rich diversity of beliefs and traditions that abound in our global city. Seeking to embrace that diversity will help us to keep afloat rather than drowning in the Sea of the Divine in which we are all immersed.

Further Reading:

Marcus J. Borg, ***The God We Never Knew,*** HarperSan Francisco, 1998

Marcus J. Borg, ed, ***Jesus at 2000,*** Westview Press, 1998

John Bowden, ***Jesus: The Unanswered Questions,*** SCM Press, London, 1998

Don Cupitt, ***The Sea of Faith: Christianity in Change*** British Broadcasting Corporation, London, 1984

Lloyd Geering, ***Tomorrow's God: How We Create Our Worlds*** (Bridget Williams Books, Wellington, New Zealand, 1994)

Langdon Gilkey, ***Society and the Sacred: Toward a Theology of Culture in Decline,*** Crossroad Publishers, New York, 1981

Charles Hartshorne, *Omnipotence and Other Theological Mistakes,* State University of New York, 1984

Philip Hammond, ed., *The Sacred in a Secular Age,* University of California Press, 1985

John Hick, *The Metaphor of God Incarnate,* SCM Press, London, 1993

John Hick and Paul F. Knitter, eds, *The Myth of Christian Uniqueness: Toward a Pluralistic Theology of Religions,* Orbis Books, New York, 1992

Charles H. Kraft, *Christianity in Culture: A Study in Biblical Theologizing in Cross-Cultural Perspective,* Orbis Books, New York, 1981

Sallie McFague, *Models of God: Theology for an Ecological Nuclear Age,* Fortress Press, Philadelphia, 1987

N. Ross Reat and Edmund F. Perry, *A World Theology: The Central Spiritual Reality of Humankind,* Cambridge University Press, 1991

Ninian Smart, ***Worldviews: Crosscultural Explorations of Human Beliefs,*** Charles Scribner's Sons, New York, 1983

Huston Smith, ***Forgotten Truth: The Common Vision of the World's Religions,*** HarperSanfrancisco, 1992 [1976]

Wilfred Cantwell Smith, ***The Meaning and End of Religion,*** Fortress Press, Minneapolis, 1991

Jon Sobrino, S.J., ***Christology at the Crossroads: A Latin American Approach,*** Orbis Books, New York, 1994 [1978].

Dorothy Sölle, ***Thinking About God: An Introduction to Theology,*** SCM Press, London and Trinity Press International, Philadelphia, 1990

Paul Tillich, ***Dynamics of Faith,*** Harper and Row, 1957

Harry J. Fielding

JUST JESUS: A Model For Our Time

That's The Spirit!

My friend, you have an inquiring mind. Otherwise you would not have read this far! Let me take your inquiring mind with me on a journey in an imaginary time-travel machine. Before you agree, let me warn you that I am not altogether in charge of this machine. It may stop wherever it chooses, in no apparent logical pattern. However, by the time we have finished our journey, I hope that you will have been able to see not only where we have been, but also some possibilities to help you plan your future. Before you climb aboard, I need to tell you that we go on this journey simply as observers, but even as we observe we will be doing so through eyes that see from our own worldview. We should try to be aware of our preconceptions and biases, but we can never fully escape them. It can be no other way. Climb aboard and let us commence our journey.

ABOUT TIME!

Stop 1: Dominican Republic, December 1999:

We are driving down a deeply rutted dirt road on the outskirts of Santo Domingo. We come to a cluster of houses—more like huts really, with walls fashioned from discarded lumber, pieces of plastic and old rusting iron. Some have thatched grass for their walls. At the far end of the village is a small wooden structure which has obviously been designated as a church; it has a rough wooden cross attached to the small door at the front. Someone has run some makeshift electrical wiring to the building which is lit by a a single bare dim light bulb. We enter the building and are greeted by the lay pastor for the small 'congregation' which consists of 2 or 3 extended families. Word has spread that some gringos are visiting this night and every available seat is taken. People are standing at the back and even spilling out through the open door. There are at least 30 people crowded into this small room which measures approximately 10 feet by 15 feet.

The service commences. We are formally welcomed by the pastor, we sing some hymns and we share in the spoken word. A lady rises to her feet and comes forward to stand in the small space between the lectern and the congregation. She begins to spin around on the hard dirt floor, twirling slowly at first and then faster and faster. As she spins she intones some words which I cannot understand. The congregation joins in, clapping and chanting as she twirls. Finally she slips to the floor and lies there in a semi-comatose state. She is helped to her feet and begins to talk in a strange tongue which is unknown to the congregation. A man in the congregation begins to 'interpret' for her, but it is obvious that he is not really listening to what she is saying. Both of them grow more frenzied and the volume of their voices rises. The general tenor of the 'interpretation' is that of chastisement. The congregation needs to repent and turn to God. If they do not do so, God will withdraw from their presence.

Others begin twirling and speaking in tongues. Finally the hubbub subsides and we share together in prayer. After a brief time of fellowship together, we gringoes take our leave.

Stop 2: France, May 30, 1431

I'm not sure where we are. I guess it is somewhere in France. I recognize the language being spoken as French, although there are some words that I do not know. Ah, of course! By the clothing and the architecture that I can see, this is probably medieval France. No wonder the language seems a bit different from my 20th century French!

There is a huge crowd of people in the distance. We walk toward the people, curious as to what is happening. As we draw closer, we can see a figure tied to a stake, surrounded by a pile of firewood. This must be an execution—perhaps a traitor or an enemy to the king. Perhaps even a heretic who has earned the displeasure of the church. There is a banner being waved by someone in the crowd—we can just make it out. On one side of the banner are the words "Jesus Maria" and a figure seated on clouds and holding a glove. Slowly the person holding the banner turns around. On the other side of the banner is a figure, probably of the virgin Mary. There is also a shield with two angels supporting the arms of France.

People all around are sobbing. Slowly, as we begin to ask some questions, and with some difficulty decipher the answers, we realize that what we are seeing is the execution of Joan of Arc. We look at each other and begin to share our scanty knowledge of Joan's history—how she was only 13 when she had her first heavenly vision; how she claimed that she was often in communication with St. Catherine and St. Margaret. These two saints had commanded her to go to the Dauphin, the designated king of France and instruct him to go to battle to win back the French city of Orleans from the English. Joan was a young woman of great piety and devotion, who inspired an entire army. It's strange, but even as we watch the executioners preparing to light the fire underneath her, we cannot help but think of Joan in the past tense.

Turning to one of the bystanders who is overcome with grief, we try to console her. "It's all right," I say. "Even though Joan is being executed as a heretic, in 500 years time she will be canonized as a saint by the church."

ABOUT TIME!

The woman just looks at me blankly through her tears. Shaking her head sorrowfully, she turns away.

As the flames now begin to lick around the ankles and knees of Joan, a misunderstood medieval spirit-person, we cannot stand to watch, and we hurry back to our time machine.

Stop 3: Approximately 30 C.E., Jerusalem

It seems to be our day for crowds! I cannot understand the languages that I hear all around me. It seems that there are many different languages being spoken. As I draw nearer to the crowd, I can hear someone talking in English. What is more, he is talking with a New Zealand accent! He is talking about God, and about Jesus. My goodness, it is the apostle Peter. This must be the day of Pentecost! But he is talking about being in the last days. He is quoting from the prophet Joel, and applying those prophecies to his own day. How funny—there has just been a rash of millennium fever in my own lifetime. People there have been predicting the end of the world in the near future. Many of them have been quoting scriptures to 'prove' that we are living in the end-times. I guess the only difference is that in my day we don't have to wait for God to destroy the world; we humans have the technology to do it by ourselves.

There's no doubt this Peter is a powerful speaker. People are coming forward in droves to ask to be baptized. Obviously some of them have had a profound spiritual experience. I'm strongly tempted to ask for baptism myself, but I've already been baptized in 1930 year's time. Hmm—I wonder what Peter's policy is on rebaptism.

Stop 4: Lamoni, Iowa, January 2000

We are in a lecture room at Graceland University. There is a theology colloquy in progress. The colloquy is open to members of the public as well as students from the college. The current speaker is focussing upon the inadequacies of orthodox theology. He states that the concept of a God 'out there', removed physically and spiritually from the world in which we live, is no longer a viable concept. He prefers a theological viewpoint known as 'panentheism' in which the entire universe is filled with the presence of the divine. He goes on to say that the image of Jesus Christ as a 'spiritual super-hero' who swooped down from some mystical 'other-world' and disguised himself as a human must be thrown into the 'spiritual trash can.' "Such a God, and such a Christ," the speaker passionately intones, "remove from us the responsibility to live in the power of the sacred and to take full responsibility to use that power to transform our personal lives and the world in which we live." There is no doubt, the speaker emphasizes, that Jesus was a 'spirit-person.' He was immersed in the power of the sacred, and expressed that power in his life and ministry. But let us not turn him into a metaphysical God, or his life becomes meaningless for us.

Many heads are nodding in agreement as the speaker concludes his remarks. I am nodding myself, but of course I dare not disagree. The speaker at the podium is me! Most of the college students are showing by their body language and their subsequent questions that they are intrigued and in general agreement with what they have heard. A few of the older participants seem somewhat uneasy and perturbed. They avoid making eye contact with the speaker. They are, however, vastly outnumbered by those who are supportive of the speaker's remarks.

Stop 5: Back to the Present

Our brief journey into time illustrates that throughout the ages people have been tuned into 'the world of spirit'. They have experienced it in various ways and expressed their experience in a wide variety of forms. For Christians, the most profound example of a 'spirit-person' was Jesus Christ.

Jesus was not unique in his perception and expressive disclosure of the world of spirit. He was part of a charismatic stream within Judaism that both preceded and followed him. There were numerous spirit-persons operating in the time of Jesus, especially around Galilee. Two of the most famous of these were Honi the Circle Drawer and Hanina ben Dosa. Of course, the public ministry of Jesus as an adult began with him being baptized by another renowned spirit-person, John the Baptist. All four gospels, as well as the book of Acts testify that there was a remarkable spirit-experience at

ABOUT TIME!

the baptism of Jesus. The book of Acts testifies that the early Christian community was also 'spirit-filled'. The Apostle Paul, in particular, apparently experienced some remarkable manifestations of the spirit.

The importance of Jesus as a spirit-person, lies not so much in the miraculous *acts* that he performed. Although it is difficult to establish which of the many accounts of miracles, healings and casting out of demons attributed to Jesus can be regarded as historically accurate, there seems little doubt that Jesus was extensively involved in such activities. The important principle that is underlined is not that Jesus was unique, but that he participated in the widespread cultural and religious ethos of his time. For Jesus and his contemporaries the world of spirit and the world of time and space were not separate worlds, but rather were different dimensions of the one world in which they lived. The question for the Jews in Jesus' time was how one gained access to the spirit dimension.

The religious leaders of Jesus time taught that access to God's blessings came from faithful observance to temple worship and from obedience to the law. The High Priests and rabbis had, in effect, become the arbitrators of how one gained access to God. Jesus and other spirit-persons sought to demonstrate in their lives and teachings that access to God came not so much by observance to the law, but by living in close relationship to the spiritual foundation of reality. This is an extremely difficult concept for us to grasp, conditioned as we are by the secular worldview of our times that has, quite rightly I believe, dismissed the dualism of earlier times and rejected the notion of a separate spiritual world and a God 'out there' who sometimes appears to intervene and sometimes does not. Such intervention, when it does appear to occur, is often in a capricious, judgmental and haphazard manner. It creates a relationship of co-dependency between the mere humans who depend upon supernatural intervention, and the interventionist God who needs and craves our obedience and worship.

Jesus' miracles must be measured against his understanding of the divine. It is true that he alluded to God at times as ***Abba*** ('father'), but that was one of many different ways that he understood the expression of the divine in human experience. ***Abba*** was a ***metaphor*** for God (God is sometimes ***like*** a father, or ***acts*** as a father would act in his best moments). Unfortunately, the almost exclusive usage of the term 'Father" for God in modern Christian, thought creates an impression of a kindly human-like figure, sitting 'out there' somewhere in the deepest recesses of space (if indeed there are such things as 'recesses' in the space-time continuum - perhaps God is hiding in one of the 'black holes' that were discovered in the 20th century). This view of God as 'Father' is extremely unhelpful and quite limiting, and really very different from the much broader view that Jesus and his contemporaries had of God. No wonder that Generation X (and many of us 'baby boomers') are turned off by the concept of such a God!

Sallie McFague, in her excellent book, ***Models of God*** (see reference at end of essay), points to other biblical metaphors for God: God as ***mother***, God as ***lover***, God as ***friend***, and the ***world as God's body***. There are of course, many references to God as ***king*** or ***lord***, and God as ***warrior*** (all of these male, hierarchical models having been appropriated by modern Christianity to refer to Jesus-and if you would dispute the last, simply recall such well known hymns as **Onward Christian Soldiers** and **Soldiers of Christ, Arise**). There are also non-personal metaphors, such as rock, and my favorite, **ruach** ('wind' or 'breath'). God as **ruach**, arose spontaneously from within creation. **Ruach** did not in the least suggest an interventionist God who lived outside the physical world.

The Hebrew world view, in many respects was very similar to the view that panentheists would call us to today. God, or the divine, pervaded the entire universe, or as a modern day process theologian, Charles Hartshorne prefers to express it, all things are in God. It was out of this worldview, that Jesus and the apostles performed their 'miracles'. Jesus understood that, in a sense, everything was divine. Of course, divinity could be 'defiled' by certain actions or attitudes, but God was 'one'-that is to say God pervaded everything. Everything was inter-related; and true *shalom* could only be achieved when every aspect of the relationship was in balance. **Shalom**, therefore meant far more than the somewhat wishy-washy 'peace' which is the usual translation in English. True *shalom* was only achieved when the entire universe was in harmony. 'Miracles' were those events which arose out of the divine ethos and helped to restore harmony.

Now there will be those who will object to the view presented above, as being too simplistic and one-sided. Quite rightly so. If all things were in the divine and the divine was acting to bring all things into harmonious relationship (to create a true ***shalom***), how do we account for the God of wrath, of war and of stern judgment that we see portrayed in various places in the bible. Christians are often prone to portray this God as an 'Old Testament' god of who demanded fear as opposed to the New Testament God of love, but as Hyam Maccoby points out (pp 205,206 - see reference at end of this chapter), the Old Testament is also replete with references to God's mercy and love. But in case I am thought to be sidestepping the issue, let me admit that some vestiges of this view remained in Jesus' day, and indeed can be found in the beliefs of more than a few fundamentalist Christians today.

Harry J. Fielding

The Sacred Kindom

No, its not a typo! And yes, Jesus did frequently refer to the 'kingdom' of God. But by the end of this essay you will see why I prefer 'kindom' to refer to the concept that was central to the life and ministry of Jesus.

There were two primary aspects that stand out from the teaching of Jesus about the kingdom. The first was that the kingdom was yet to come and would signal the triumph of God and God's rule over the world. This aspect is termed the ***eschatological*** teaching, eschatology having to do with the 'end-times' or final stages of the world. The second aspect was that the kingdom was *now:* "the kingdom of God is among [or in the midst] of you" (Luke, 17: 20-1), "the kingdom of God has come upon you" (Matthew, 12:28; Luke, 11:20). Interestingly, this is one of the very few references that Matthew has to the 'kingdom of God'- mostly he refers to the 'kingdom of heaven', possibly because he did not want to upset his Jewish readers by using the word 'God". In effect, what Jesus was saying is that ***his*** life was a model for how the kingdom was to operate.

ABOUT TIME!

It was clear that Jesus was expecting/promoting an earthly kingdom. The words of the 'Lord's prayer' emphasize this when they talk about God's kingdom coming *on earth*, just as it (the kingdom) is in heaven. There seems little doubt that Jesus' understanding of the Hebrew *shalom* was a foundational influence in his concept of the kingdom. In fact, as many scholars have pointed out, the term 'kingdom of God' can in most instances be equally validly translated as the 'rule of God'. When God's rule is truly established, true harmony (or *shalom*) will be found. When this harmony is in place, there will be a recognition of the interrelatedness of all things. If we are related to all things we are *kin* to them—hence we can talk about the time of God's rule as ***God's kindom***, where we acknowledge our kinship under God. Remembering again that Jesus' understanding of 'God' was far broader than the orthodox Christian concept tends to be, rather than speak of 'God's kingdom', I think the relatedness and sacredness of all of life is better understood by using the term 'the sacred kindom'.

Harry J. Fielding

What did Jesus teach about the kindom?

Jesus was a descendant of generations of forbears who had developed a belief in the relatedness of life and the sovereignty of God. The earliest expressions of God were quite tribal in nature and tied to the land and the people. The early God of Israel was simply regarded as one of many tribal gods. Unless we understand this, we do not understand the reference in the Hebrew *shema* "Beware, lest your heart be deceived, and you turn and serve other gods, and worship them." Gradually over the centuries the concept of God and the kingdom of God broadened out to include non-Israelites. God (Yahweh) was imbued with characteristics such as love, righteousness and holiness. A *relational* God had begun to emerge and it was this aspect of God which was predominant in Jesus' view of the kingdom. As my colleague and good friend, David Heinze expresses it,

> *The powers of the 'age to come' had invaded the 'present age' in Jesus' ministry. Jesus, however, denied any precise knowledge as to the time of the*

ABOUT TIME!

full manifestation of God's reign in Mark 13:32[4].

The 'manifesto' attributed to Jesus in the fourth chapter of the gospel of Luke, where he quotes from the prophet Isaiah, sets out the view that Jesus' ministry was centered in the spirit: "The Spirit of the Lord is upon me." It also focuses upon service and ministry in the present world. The captives to be delivered, the blind who are to have their sight restored, the prisoners who are to be set free are all residents of the present world and their liberation cannot wait until the next world. Jesus' relationship to the Spirit, as Marcus Borg points out, was "an intense experiential relationship"[5] and it was really the living out of relationships within the power of the Spirit which informed Jesus' understanding of the kingdom of God.

The synoptic gospels (Matthew, Mark and Luke) clearly capture the existential nature of Jesus' kingdom ministry as well as the future manifestation awaiting fulfillment. The fourth

---

[4] David M. Heinze, unpublished paper, "The Kingdom of God", January, 2000.
[5] Marcus J. Borg, *Jesus: A New Vision,* Harper SanFrancisco, page 45

gospel (John), however, and passages in Acts, appear to shift the emphasis to the coming of a future kingdom. The early disciples seemed to be expecting the imminent return of Jesus and their focus was on the idea of Jesus as the crucified and risen messiah who would shortly be returning in great power. This theme grew more pronounced in Christian history with the passing of time, until eventually an elaborate system of church government was established and the church became the vehicle by which Christian disciples gained access to Jesus and God.

The Relevance of the Sacred Kindom Today

We live in a broken and divided world. Yet this brokenness and division are not the essential and natural attributes of the world. As suggested in the previous essay, we are connected together in the Sea of the Divine. The separation and brokenness which we find, exists because we deny our unity and connectedness and try to operate as separate and discrete entities in the world of which we are actually a component part. In orthodox Christian terminology, we call this desire to choose a broken and divided state, "sin." Sin is anything that causes us to lose our connection to the sacred, including to each other. The 'sacred' and the 'secular' are not separate entities but are simply different dimensions of God, as we understand the model of the universe as God's body.

It is when we recognize our connectedness with all of life, that we can most clearly resonate with the ministry and call of Jesus and can see the relevance of the sacred kindom in our day and age. When we ignore the suffering of others, when we turn a blind eye to injustice and exploitation, when we insist individually or collectively that our "rights" are more important than other people or other aspects of the world in which we live, then we do great harm to God's body and because we are part of that body, we unwittingly do great harm to ourselves.

It is only when we understand that the nature of the universe (indeed the essential nature of life itself) is spiritual that we can truly begin to put the problems of the world into perspective and in our common unity begin to work in unity to promote the common good. If the words of the well-known Christian

Harry J. Fielding

song, ***We Are One in the Spirit*** are to be more than simply empty rhetoric, we must see the life and example of Jesus calling us to be a people of ***Justice,*** united together in the power of the Spirit and sensing our connectedness in the Sea of the Divine. We ***do*** travel in a time machine: this fragile planet that we call home. Our life and actions are connected to those who have gone before us and with those who follow. Our calling is to live together in harmony in the power of the sacred. When that happens, the sacred kindom is already here. Let's change this world for the better!

IT'S ABOUT TIME!

REFERENCES AND FURTHER READING:

Marcus J. Borg, *Jesus—A New Vision. Spirit, Culture and the Life of Discipleship*, Harper SanFrancisco, 1987

Charles Hartshorne, *Omnipotence and Other Theological Mistakes* (Suny Press, 1984)

Sallie McFague, *Models of God: Theology for an Ecological Nuclear Age* (Fortress Press, Philadelphia, 1988)

Hyam Maccoby, *Revolution in Judea: Jesus and the Jewish Resistance* (Taplinger Publishing Co., New York, 1973)

Robert Mesle, *Process Theology: A Basic Introduction* (Chalice Press, St Louis, 1993 [part 3 is especially relevant to the above essay])

John Shelby Spong, *Rescuing the Bible from Fundamentalism* (Harper, San Francisco, 1991 [see especially chapters 2 and 14])

Harry J. Fielding

Nathan Stone, ***Names of God*** (Moody Press, Chicago, 1944)

ABOUT THE AUTHOR

Harry James Fielding was born more years ago than he cares to remember, in Auckland, New Zealand. He was educated at the University of Auckland, St. Johns Theological College, and the University of Queensland in Brisbane, Australia.

Harry was once an avid competitive sportsman, but currently his activities are restricted to snow skiing, slow jogging, a little canoeing and some recreational tennis.

Harry resides in Orlando Florida and works as a missionary/administrator assigned to the Caribbean including Haiti, the most economically impoverished country in the western hemisphere. He finds his work both enjoyable and challenging.

Harry has a long-time interest in writing and has been published in poetry anthologies, skiing magazines and in church and theology journals.

Printed in the United States
21659LVS00001B/100-138